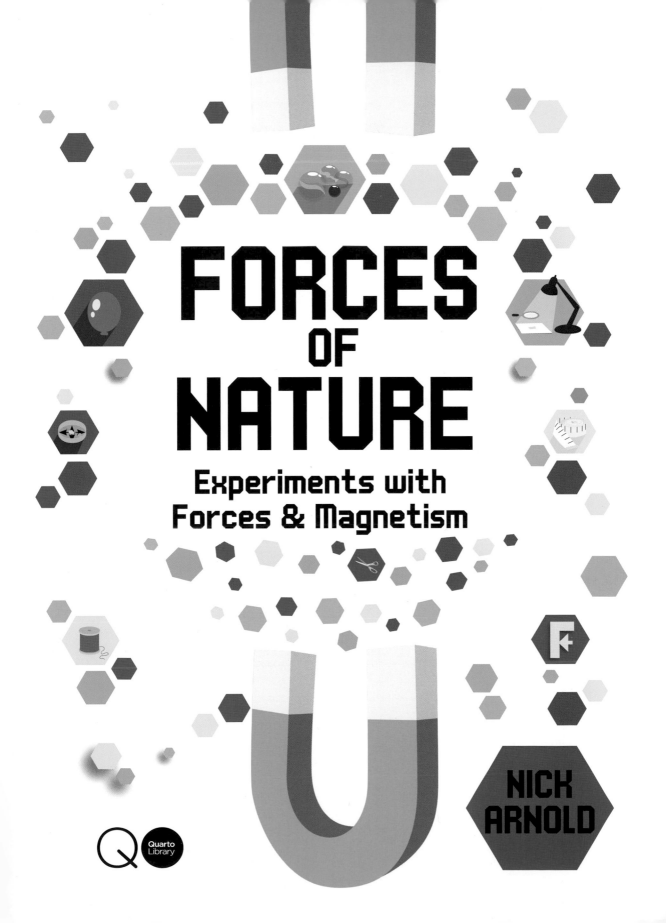

FORCES
OF
NATURE

Experiments with
Forces & Magnetism

NICK ARNOLD

Quarto
Library

Quarto is the authority on a wide range of topics.

Quarto educates, entertains and enriches the lives of our readers—enthusiasts and lovers of hands-on living.

www.quartoknows.com

Publisher: Maxime Boucknooghe
Editorial Director: Victoria Garrard
Art Director: Miranda Snow
Project editor: Sophie Hallam
Design and Editorial: Cloud King Creative
Consultant: Pete Robinson
CSciTeach of the Association for Science Education

This library edition published in 2019 by Quarto Library,
an imprint of The Quarto Group.
6 Orchard Road, Suite 100
Lake Forest, CA 92630
T: +1 949 380 7510
F: +1 949 380 7575
www.QuartoKnows.com

A CIP record for this book is available from the Library of Congress.

ISBN 978 0 71124 227 2

Manufactured in Dongguan, China TL012019

9 8 7 6 5 4 3 2 1

MIX
Paper from
responsible sources
FSC® C104723

CONTENTS

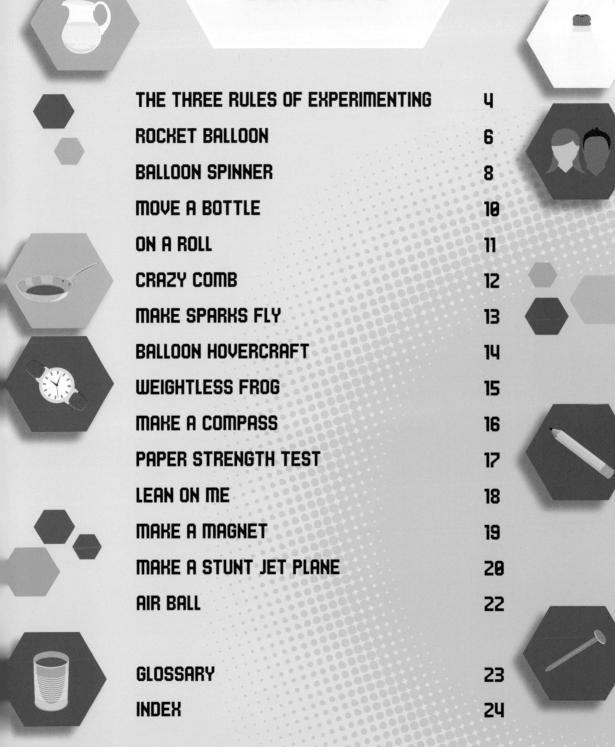

THE THREE RULES OF EXPERIMENTING

RULE #1

BE ORGANIZED

Before you start the experiment, read the WHAT YOU NEED list of materials and equipment. Make sure you have everything you need. If you go off in search of something halfway through an experiment, it may not be safe and it might ruin your results. If you can't find what you need, feel free to use a similar item, but ALWAYS ask before you borrow anything!

All great scientists know the three golden rules of experimenting. These rules show you how to experiment safely and happily.

RULE #2

BE SAFE

This is a book for safe scientists. Adult supervision is always needed with experiments. Pay attention to all the DANGER warnings. In particular, NEVER drink or eat an experiment unless this book says you can.

• BEWARE of sharp pins and scissors.
• BEWARE of hot batteries—if a battery gets hot, disconnect it immediately.

This book doesn't need mains electricity, fire, or harmful chemicals—so don't use them in your experiments!

RULE #3

BE CLEAN

Be careful not to spill messy materials like water or food coloring. Always clean up before you start a new experiment. Cleaning up sounds seriously boring, but it helps you. Yes, really! Cleaning up:

- Clears space for your next experiment.
- Keeps you from losing vital equipment.
- Keeps younger kids from playing with your experiments and hurting themselves or breaking your equipment.
- Means you won't get grounded and banned from experimenting!

WHAT'S NEXT?

Look out for the "What's Next?" challenge. Search for clues to explore and develop the experiments in the book—and find the answers for yourselves! See if you can set up your own lab area at home, with a box for your lab equipment. You could keep a notebook with the results of your experiments.

ROCKET BALLOON

You'll be amazed to discover that a balloon filled with air can blast along just like a rocket!

WHAT YOU DO

1. Set up the two chairs six yards apart.

2. Cut 20 feet of string. Tie one end of the string to the top of one of the chairs.

3. Thread the straw through the string and tie the other end of the string to the top of the second chair.

4. Blow up the balloon and let it go three times. Blow it up a fourth time and secure it to the straw with tape while holding the balloon neck closed.

5. Set up the experiment so the balloon neck is close to one chair and then let the balloon go.

QUIZ QUESTION:

WHAT WILL HAPPEN TO THE BALLOON?

A) THE BALLOON WHIZZES TO THE FAR END OF THE STRING

B) THE BALLOON REACHES THE FAR END AND MOVES BACK ALONG THE STRING

C) THE BALLOON POPS

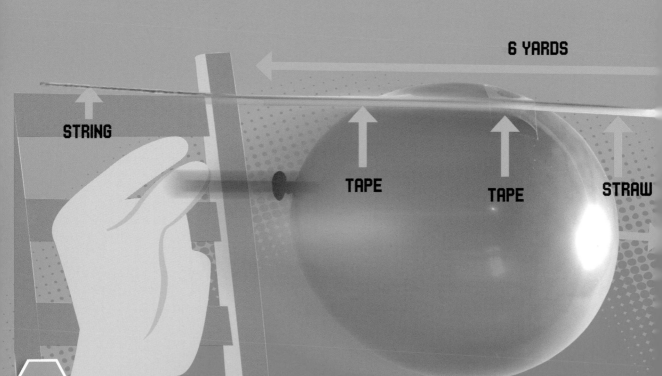

6 YARDS

STRING

TAPE

TAPE

STRAW

ANSWER: A

When you compress air in the balloon, the air pushes back. Sir Isaac Newton's third law of motion shows that any force creates an equal force in the opposite direction.

This is why air blasting backward from the balloon pushes the balloon forward.

WHAT'S NEXT?

Repeat the experiment twice, each time with less air in the balloon. How does this affect the balloon's speed and travel distance?

WHAT YOU NEED

Balloon

2 chairs

Tape

Measuring tape

Scissors

Drinking straw

String

DID YOU KNOW?

Rockets and jet engines work like your experiment. The force comes from burning fuel and hot gases, which are blasted backward. This propels the rocket or jet forward.

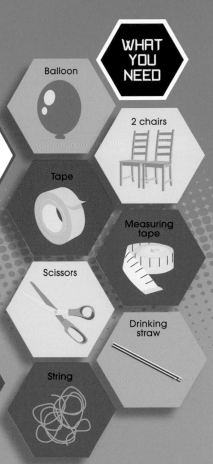

7

BALLOON SPINNER

Why waste effort spinning balloons with your hands when all you need is magnetism!

WHAT YOU DO

1 Arrange the magnets in a line so that their ends all stick together. If the ends push apart, just turn one magnet around so that they line up.

2 One by one, take four magnets from your line without turning them and tape them to the balloon. Stick the bar magnets in a level, evenly-spaced line all the way around the balloon.

3 Tie 30 inches of string to the balloon. Ask an adult helper to press the pin through the other end of the string and attach it to the top of a door.

4 Take the remaining magnet and, without turning it, stroke the air alongside, but not touching, one of the balloon magnets.

5 Turn your magnet so it points in the opposite direction. Repeat Step 4.

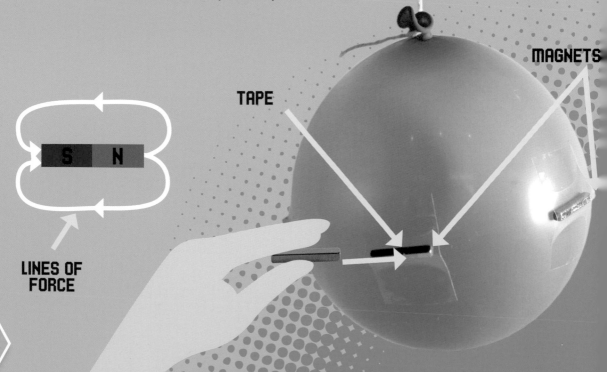

MAGNETS

TAPE

S   N

LINES OF FORCE

WHAT HAPPENS?

ANSWER: A

Every magnet has a north and south pole. Its magnetic field has magnetic lines of force that leave the north pole and re-enter the south pole. Opposite poles attract, but the same poles push apart.

You start the balloon with a push from your handheld magnet. The alternate pull and push on passing balloon magnets keeps the balloon turning.

WHAT YOU NEED

Balloon

String

Scissors

Measuring tape

5 bar magnets

Wide tape

Push pin

WHAT'S NEXT?

Repeat Steps 1–3 with another balloon, but this time ensure the magnets point the opposite way to the magnets on the first balloon. What happens when you hang the two balloons together?

DID YOU KNOW?

Electric motors use magnets and electricity to produce motion.

MOVE A BOTTLE

This is a great party trick to impress your friends. Just don't forget to keep the bottle cap on!

WHAT YOU DO

1. Use the pencil to make a small hole in the cardstock, 1 inch from the bottom.

2. Cut 33 inches of string and tie a knot through the hole.

3. Place the cardstock on a smooth table and the bottle on top of the cardstock. Don't open the bottle.

4. Gently pull the string, then give the string a quick tug.

INERTIA

FRICTION BETWEEN THE BOTTLE AND PAPER

WHAT YOU NEED

Pencil

16 fl oz. plastic bottle of water

Scissors

8½" x 11" cardstock

String

Ruler

Table

Sandpaper

QUIZ QUESTION:

WHAT WILL HAPPEN WHEN YOU TUG THE STRING?

A) THE BOTTLE FLIES THROUGH THE AIR

B) THE BOTTLE FALLS ON THE FLOOR—LUCKY I LEFT THE CAP ON!

C) THE BOTTLE DOESN'T MOVE

WHAT HAPPENS?

ANSWER: C

Inertia tries to keep the bottle where it is. But **friction** between the bottle and the cardstock tries to keep the bottle on the cardstock.

When you pull the string gently, friction wins and the bottle moves with the cardstock. But the friction is weak. A rapid tug on the string overcomes friction and inertia keeps the bottle where it is.

WHAT'S NEXT?

Try sticking sandpaper over the cardstock. Why won't the experiment work?

ON A ROLL

When balls bump and bash into each other, it's the science of momentum that's all-important ....

WHAT YOU NEED

- 8½" x 11" cardstock
- Tape measure
- Books to stack 5 in. high.
- Scissors
- Modeling clay
- Marbles (or other balls of different sizes)

WHAT YOU DO

1. Fold the cardstock in half lengthwise and cut along the fold. You should be left with two pieces, each about 4 inches wide.

2. Fold each side of each piece of cardstock in 1 inch to make U-shaped channels.

3. Set up the experiment as shown, with a blob of modeling clay under the channel to hold it in place.

4. Place the small marble at the base of the slope and roll the large marble from the top. Swap the marbles around and repeat.

QUIZ QUESTION:

WHAT WILL HAPPEN?

A) THE LITTLE MARBLE KNOCKS THE BIG MARBLE FARTHER

B) THE BIG MARBLE KNOCKS THE LITTLE MARBLE FARTHER

C) THE LITTLE MARBLE HITS THE BIG MARBLE AND REBOUNDS UP THE RAMP

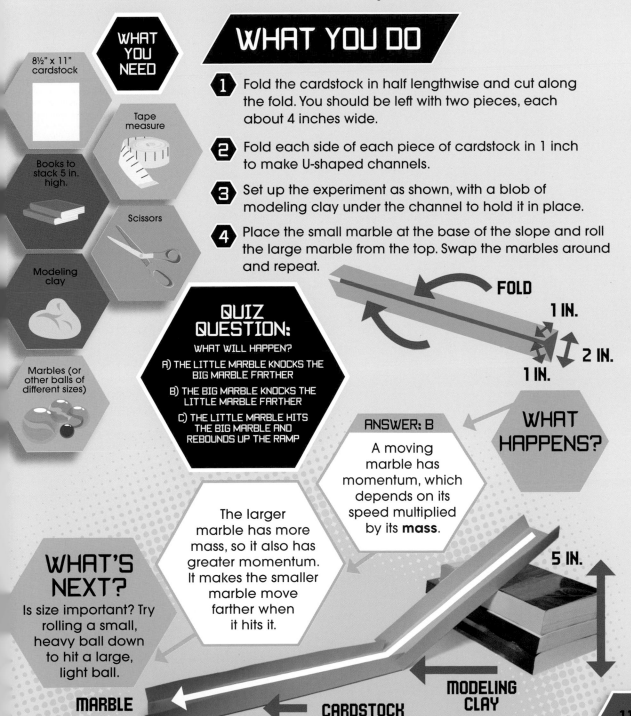

FOLD
1 IN.
2 IN.
1 IN.

ANSWER: B

A moving marble has momentum, which depends on its speed multiplied by its **mass**.

WHAT HAPPENS?

The larger marble has more mass, so it also has greater momentum. It makes the smaller marble move farther when it hits it.

WHAT'S NEXT?

Is size important? Try rolling a small, heavy ball down to hit a large, light ball.

5 IN.

MARBLE

CARDSTOCK CHANNEL

MODELING CLAY

CRAZY COMB

Combing your hair sends your electrons off on an exciting scientific journey!

Your hair
(must be clean
and dry)

Small plate

Teaspoon

Honey

Clean, dry
comb

WHAT YOU DO

1 Comb your hair quickly 20–30 times.

2 Collect a little honey on the back of the spoon. Trickle a thin stream of honey onto the plate.

3 Now hold the comb close to the honey stream and near the spoon.

QUIZ QUESTION:

WHAT WILL HAPPEN TO THE HONEY STREAM?

A) IT FORMS A SPIRAL

B) IT BENDS

C) IT STOPS AND STARTS

WHAT HAPPENS?

ANSWER: B

Combing your hair gives the comb an electric **charge**. This is because your hair transfers electrons to it. The charge on the comb attracts uncharged objects, such as the stream of honey.

The charge on the comb pushes electrons in the honey away and attracts the positive charge that is left.

WHAT'S NEXT?

Repeat the experiment with a thin stream of water from a faucet. How do you explain your result?

MAKE SPARKS FLY

Here's how to make your own lightning, in perfect safety!

WHAT YOU DO

1 Darken the room. It also needs to be a dry evening.

2 Rub the balloon on the rug or blanket 250 times firmly and very fast.

3 Put the spoon up to the balloon. You should see a tiny flash between the two. That's a spark.

QUIZ QUESTION:

WHAT CAUSES THE SPARK?

A) ELECTRONS LEAP FROM SPOON TO BALLOON

B) ELECTRONS LEAP FROM BALLOON TO SPOON

C) IT'S ELECTRICITY FROM MY BODY

WHAT HAPPENS?

ANSWER: B

The charge on the balloon cannot move until you bring a metal object close to it. The charge can jump across a small gap as a spark and travel down the metal because metals conduct electricity.

DID YOU KNOW?

When lightning strikes, electrons leap between the clouds and Earth. Lightning is over 54,000°F. The heat boosts **air pressure**, causing a shockwave that we hear as thunder.

13

BALLOON HOVERCRAFT

Here's how to float objects on a cushion of air!

WHAT YOU DO

1. Stretch the balloon neck over one end of the spool.
2. Stick the other end of the spool to the CD with a ring of modeling clay.
3. Blow up the balloon from the CD end. Hold the balloon neck so air doesn't escape.
4. Place the CD on a smooth surface and then release the balloon.

WHAT YOU NEED

Spool of thread

Unwanted CD

Balloon

Modeling clay

SPOOL

MODELING CLAY

QUIZ QUESTION:

WHAT WILL HAPPEN TO THE CD?

A) THE CD TAKES OFF LIKE A FLYING SAUCER

B) THE CD SPINS ON THE SPOT VERY FAST

C) THE CD MOVES AROUND

WHAT HAPPENS?

ANSWER: C

Air escaping from the balloon forms a layer between the CD and the surface, reducing friction. This enables the CD to hover slightly and move easily across a smooth surface.

DID YOU KNOW?

Like your hovercraft, a real hovercraft floats on a cushion of air. The hovercraft was invented in 1956 by Christopher Cockerell following tests with old cans and a hair dryer!

WEIGHTLESS FROG

Can magnetism really make a frog float in mid-air?

WHAT YOU NEED

- Pencil
- Tape
- 2 bar magnets
- Scissors
- Ruler
- Paper
- Colored pencils

WHAT YOU DO

1 Draw a dotted line ½ inch from the longer edge of the paper. Draw a frog above this line, as shown. Color it in and fold down along the dotted line so that it stands up.

2 Place one magnet on the table and put the pencil sideways on top of it. Place the other magnet on top of the pencil. Check that the magnets push each other away and then join them together with tape.

3 Remove the pencil. Stand the frog on the top magnet. Your frog will now float in mid-air!

QUIZ QUESTION:

WHY DOES THE FROG APPEAR TO FLOAT?

A) THE MAGNETS REPEL EACH OTHER

B) THE FROG HAS SUPER POWERS

C) THE FROG IS LIGHTER THAN AIR

WHAT HAPPENS?

ANSWER: A
The south pole and north pole of a magnet attract each other, but two north poles and two south poles repel each other. The bottom magnet pushes the top magnet and the frog away, and that's why it appears to float.

DID YOU KNOW?

In 1997, scientists made a real frog float in a strong magnetic field. The frog was unharmed.

15

MAKE A COMPASS

Feeling lost? Here's a science experiment to guide you home.

WHAT YOU DO

1 Stroke the pin with the magnet 50 times in the same direction. Stick the pin in the plastic cap with modeling clay.

2 Float the plastic cap in the bowl of water and note which way the pin points.

3 Use the map to find north located at the top.

WHAT YOU NEED

Pin

Modeling clay

Plastic bottle cap (about 1½ in. across)

Bowl of water

Magnet

Local map

CAP

PIN

MODELING CLAY

QUIZ QUESTION:

WHERE WILL THE PIN POINT?

A) ALWAYS NORTH

B) ALWAYS SOUTH

C) SOMETIMES NORTH AND SOMETIMES SOUTH

WHAT HAPPENS?

ANSWER: A

Earth is a giant magnet. When you stroked the pin with the magnet, you turned the pin into a magnet.

Now your magnetic pin lines up with Earth's magnetic field.

WHAT'S NEXT?

What happens if you put a magnet close to your compass? Does it matter which pole is closest to the compass?

PAPER STRENGTH TEST

You can't support a book with just two sheets of paper . . . or can you?

WHAT YOU DO

1 Fold one piece of paper lengthwise. Cut along the fold.

2 Make two pillars by rolling two half-sheets sideways as shown. Secure the edges with tape and add rubber bands for support.

3 Fold up the second sheet of paper 1 inch from one end. Turn the paper and fold it down for the next 1 inch. Firmly fold the entire sheet up or down until the end.

4 Place the pillars 5 inches apart and place the folded paper on top. Then put a book on top of the paper.

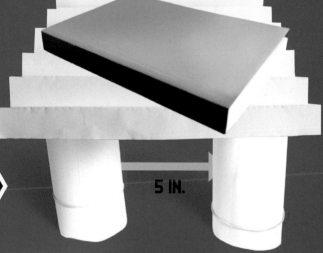

5 IN.

QUIZ QUESTION:
WHAT WILL HAPPEN?
A) THE PAPER SUPPORTS THE BOOK
B) THE BOOK SWAYS FROM SIDE TO SIDE
C) THE BOOK SQUASHES EVERYTHING

WHAT HAPPENS?

ANSWER: A
The folds in the paper make it stiff like cardboard. It will bend easily in one direction, but not the other.

Each pillar takes the force and spreads it evenly around its **circumference**.

WHAT'S NEXT?
How many books can the paper structure support? Can the pillars carry **weight** if laid on their side? If not, why not?

17

LEAN ON ME

Can you hold up the Leaning Tower of Pisa using the amazing power of force?

WHAT YOU NEED

Pen

Long cardboard tube

Ruler

Modeling clay

Felt-tip pens or paint

Scissors

WHAT YOU DO

1. Make a ½ inch vertical cut at one end of the tube.

2. Mark the tube base opposite the cut. Link your mark and the top of the cut with a curved dotted line on both sides.

3. Lay the tube down and cut along the dotted lines. You can decorate your tube like the Leaning Tower of Pisa if you'd like.

4. Stand your tower on its cut end and then blow. The leaning tower falls easily.

5. Stick a 1½ inch ball of modeling clay inside the tower on the long side. The ball should be ¼ inch above the tower base. Now try blowing again.

CUT

QUIZ QUESTION:

WHAT WILL HAPPEN WHEN YOU BLOW?

A) THE TOWER FALLS IN A DIFFERENT DIRECTION

B) THE TOWER DOESN'T FALL

C) THE TOWER TURNS AROUND

WHAT HAPPENS?

ANSWER: B

Gravity tries to pull the tower down in the direction that it leans at Step 4. It's easy to blow the tower down, especially in this direction.

A weight at the tower base pulls the tower downward and counter-balances the leaning force.

WHAT'S NEXT?

Move the weight toward the top of the tower. What happens now and why?

DID YOU KNOW?

The Leaning Tower of Pisa took 199 years to build. It leans because it was built in soft soil with shallow foundations!

MAKE A MAGNET

Don't have a magnet? That's no problem for a scientist. Here's how to make your own....

WHAT YOU NEED

- 30-35 in. of thin electrical wire
- Compass (make a compass on page 16)
- 1.5 volt battery
- Scissors
- Large steel nail or screw
- Tape

WHAT YOU DO

1. Wrap the wire around the nail many times.

2. Fasten the ends of the wire to the ends of the battery with tape, making sure bare metal is touching the battery.

3. Hold the battery, nail, and wire close to the compass.

QUIZ QUESTION:

WHAT WILL HAPPEN TO THE COMPASS?

A) THE COMPASS NEEDLE SWINGS AND STOPS

B) THE NEEDLE SPINS IN CIRCLES

C) THE COMPASS BEGINS TO HEAT UP

WHAT HAPPENS?

ANSWER: A

A magnetic field is a region where there is a magnetic force. A magnetic field forms around a wire when an electric current flows through it.

The battery makes the nail magnetic and they both affect the magnetic compass needle.

WHAT'S NEXT?

Can your magnetic nail pick up a paperclip?

WARNING!

IF THE BATTERY OR WIRE GETS HOT, DISCONNECT THE BATTERY RIGHT AWAY. DO NOT USE A RECHARGEABLE BATTERY FOR THIS EXPERIMENT.

MAKE A STUNT

Here's a fantastic scientific challenge—build and test your very own stunt jet!

WHAT YOU DO

1 Fold the cardstock lengthwise and then cut the folded cardstock as shown below, with the folded edge at the bottom.

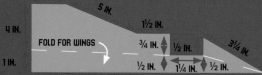

2 IN.
5 IN.
4 IN.
1½ IN.
FOLD FOR WINGS
¾ IN. ½ IN. 3¼ IN.
1 IN.
½ IN. 1¼ IN. ½ IN.

2 Fold the cardstock down along the dotted lines to make the wings. Open out the cardstock. Cut a leftover piece of cardstock like this.

1¼ IN.
4 IN.
3 IN. 1¼ IN. ¾ IN.
18 IN.

3 This will be the jet fuselage and tail fin. Place the fuselage between the wings and secure with staples. Add a paperclip as shown.

PAPERCLIP   STAPLES

4 Cut and fold the tail and wings to add **ailerons** and the rudder.

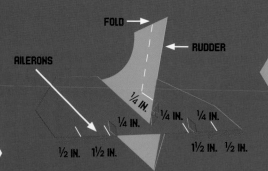

FOLD
RUDDER
AILERONS
¼ IN.
¼ IN. ¼ IN. ¼ IN.
½ IN. 1½ IN.   1½ IN. ½ IN.

20

QUIZ QUESTION:

WHAT WILL HAPPEN WHEN YOU BEND THE AILERONS UP?

A) THE PLANE FLIES UP

B) THE PLANE FLIES DOWN

C) THE PLANE LOOPS THE LOOP

WHAT HAPPENS?

ANSWER: A

Planes fly because of a force called lift caused by the air pressure under the plane. Raising ailerons increases lift and the plane flies up.

DID YOU KNOW?

Your stunt jet is a type known as "delta wing" for its wing shape. Delta wings are most commonly seen on military aircraft and are ideal for supersonic flight (faster than the **speed of sound**).

JET PLANE

WHAT'S NEXT?

Try adjusting the positions of the ailerons and rudder. How can you make the plane fly downward? Can you make one wing dip and the other lift or make the plane turn to one side?

Your plane is fast because its streamlined shape reduces friction with the air. This friction is called drag.

WHAT YOU NEED

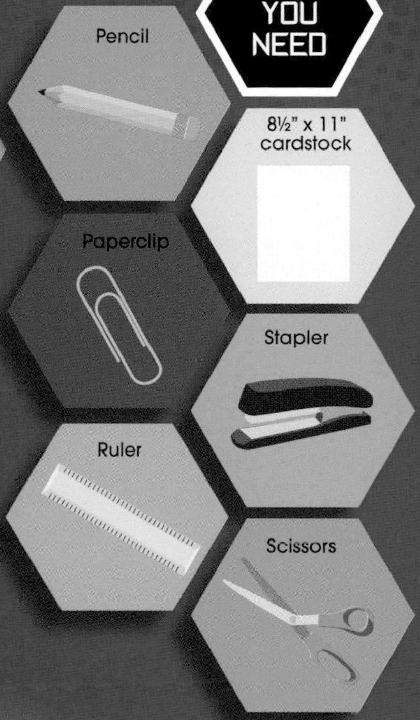

Pencil

8½" x 11" cardstock

Paperclip

Stapler

Ruler

Scissors

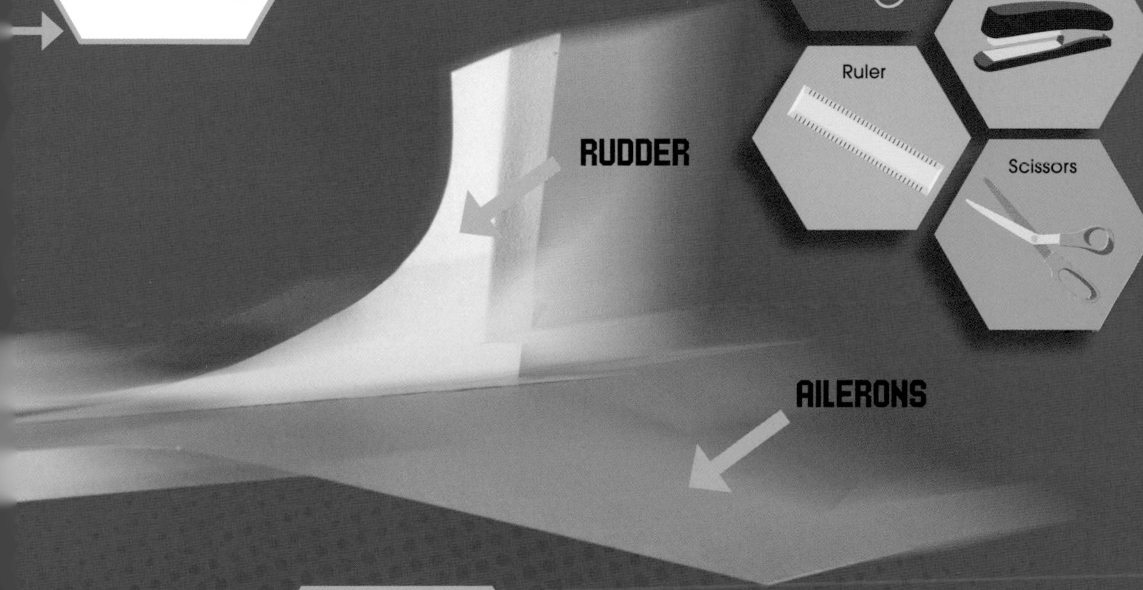

RUDDER

AILERONS

FORCE QUIZ

CAN YOU FIND THE MISSING WORDS?

1) THE QUALITY OF I _____ MAKES IT HARD TO MOVE AN OBJECT.

2) THE FORCE OF F _____ SLOWS THINGS DOWN.

3) THE FORCE OF G _____ PULLS OBJECTS TOWARD THE EARTH.

Answers:1) Inertia, 2) Friction, 3) Gravity.

AIR BALL

By combining air pressure and force, you'll have the power to move objects.

WHAT YOU NEED

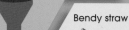

Empty 2-liter plastic bottle (with cap removed)

Styrofoam ball

Funnel (big enough for the ball to fit inside)

Bendy straw

WHAT YOU DO

1 Balance the styrofoam ball on the bottle.

2 Clap your hands on the sides of the bottle. What happens?

3 Now place the funnel in the bottle and the ball inside the funnel.

4 Repeat Step 2.

QUIZ QUESTION:

WHAT WILL HAPPEN AT STEP 4?

A) THE BALL DOESN'T GO ANYWHERE

B) THE BALL FLIES IN A FIGURE OF EIGHT

C) THE BALL HEATS UP AND STARTS STEAMING

WHAT HAPPENS?

ANSWER: A

At Step 2 the force of air pressure raises the ball. When the ball's in the funnel, the air speeds up to get around it.

Faster air has a lower pressure, and so the pressure below the ball is lower than pressure above it. The ball is held in the funnel by the air pressure of the room.

WHAT'S NEXT?

Try this experiment using a bendy straw instead of a bottle. Bend the straw and blow through the longer end. Can you make the styrofoam ball hover? Why does the ball spin?

AIR PRESSURE

AIR FLOW

AIR FLOW

GLOSSARY

Aileron
A hinged part on the back edge of an aircraft's wing that can be moved up or down to help control the aircraft's movement.

Air pressure
The force of the air pressing on something. Air pressure increases with temperature.

Atom
A particle made up of a nucleus (containing protons and neutrons), usually surrounded by electrons. It's hard to break atoms into smaller particles.

Charge
Charged objects can attract and repel each other. Inside atoms, electrons have negative charge and protons have positive charge.

Circumference
The distance around the edge of a circle (or any curved shape).

Force
A push or pull that can make an object speed up, slow down, stay still, change direction or change shape.

Friction
The force that occurs when two surfaces pass over each other.

Gravity
The force that pulls every object with mass together. On Earth, it pulls objects toward the planet's center.

Inertia
The quality that keeps an object motionless or moving in a straight line unless another force affects it.

Mass
The matter (atoms, etc.) that makes up an object.

Speed of sound
At room temperature (68° F) sound travels through air at a speed of 1,125 feet per second.

Weight
The force exerted by gravity on an object. The weight of an object changes according to gravity.

INDEX

PICTURE CREDITS

(t=top, b=bottom, l=left, r=right, c=center)

Shutterstock
7b 3Dsculptor, 9b I. Pilon, 12b jeka84, 13b Dark Moon Pictures, 14b Stephen Clarke, 15b Tsekhmister, 18b Fedor Selivanov, 20-21b Dr Ajay Kumar Singh.

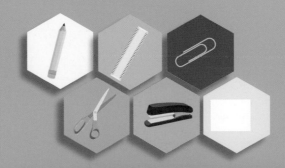